POEMS

JOURNEY
TO THE
MORNING
LIGHT

CATHERINE
DE VINCK

IRON
PEN

PARACLETE PRESS
BREWSTER, MASSACHUSETTS

2023 First Printing

Journey to the Morning Light: Poems

Copyright © 2023 by Catherine de Vinck

ISBN 978-1-64060-770-5

The Iron Pen name and logo are trademarks of Paraclete Press.

Cover art: *Morning Glory* by Pierre-Joseph Redouté (1759–1840), modified from the original, Swallowtail Garden Seeds

Library of Congress Cataloging-in-Publication Data
Names: De Vinck, Catherine, author.
Title: Journey to the morning light : poems / Catherine de Vinck.
Description: Brewster, Massachusetts : Paraclete Press, [2022] | Summary:
  "Poems of sorrow, joy, thanksgiving"-- Provided by publisher.
Identifiers: LCCN 2022019644 (print) | LCCN 2022019645 (ebook) | ISBN
  9781640607705 (trade paperback) | ISBN 9781640607712 (epub) | ISBN
  9781640607729 (pdf)
Subjects: BISAC: POETRY / Subjects & Themes / Inspirational & Religious |
  POETRY / Subjects & Themes / Nature | LCGFT: Poetry.
Classification: LCC PS3554.E928 J68 2022 (print) | LCC PS3554.E928
  (ebook) | DDC 811/.54--dc23/eng/20220422
LC record available at https://lccn.loc.gov/2022019644
LC ebook record available at https://lccn.loc.gov/2022019645

10 9 8 7 6 5 4 3 2 1

Published by Paraclete Press
Brewster, Massachusetts
www.paracletepress.com

Digitally Printed

❧ CONTENTS ❧

FOREWORD

CATHERINE DE VINCK CALLS US TO EVER GREATER awareness of who we are and where we dwell. She offers us glimpses of truth, not answers to our questions. She lights the path, sometimes with the brilliance of a single image. More often she surrounds us with the atmosphere of dusk—the twilight arising in our consciousness where mood and memory mingle.

I first met Catherine de Vinck in 1964 when I studied with her daughter, Anne Catherine, at Holy Child High School in Suffern, New York. Anne Catherine frequently invited me to her home for their family's Sunday lunch.

The de Vincks lived in a large, rambling Victorian house in Allendale, New Jersey, overflowing with books. It was a joy for me to go there. To be liberated from boarding school for an afternoon was pure bliss. Being with a big family like my own, sharing a home-cooked meal, and savoring good conversation and laughter was memorable.

My recollection of Catherine from that time was of a vibrant, smiling woman with an engaging French accent. She was married to José, a professor, scholar, and translator. When they immigrated from Belgium in 1948 after the war, she didn't know English or much about America—its society, customs, and values. Yet she sailed with José across the Atlantic to start a new life, as so many others had.

They raised six children with love, care, and grace, including their beloved Oliver, who was bedridden. With such a busy household and a husband immersed in translations of five volumes of Bonaventure's writings, it is a wonder that Catherine could find a moment to write. But she did somehow, and managed to create hundreds of poems. They became the wellspring of our friendship.

I hold in my hands some of Catherine's letters written over the years that always carried a new poem or two. I pick up her many books of poetry published by Alleluia Press, which her husband founded. The first one, *A Time to Gather,* was published in 1967 when she was 45. She continued to write poetry until she died at 99 on December 15, 2021.

I sit in wonder at what she has given to our world over these decades. Each poem carefully crafted, every thought creatively woven. How might one summarize her gifts? How shall we comment on her poetic talents and spiritual insights?

She holds her mind's eye steady to illuminate the numinous beauty of the world and the palpable mystery that infuses it. She invites us into this great presence where everything—trees and forests, water and rivers, clouds and air, plants and stones—is alive and is speaking to us. Figures emerge as night moves in and darkness holds us in its silent embrace. Fox and deer, birds and rabbits pass through her vista from the nearby woods, capturing her imagination and expanding ours. They are part of the living world where she dwells.

Yet deep silence surrounds her imagination so that her poetic images arise from a state of reverie, from moments of grace, and from sustained vigilance. Each poem is a meditation painted with words springing from the depths of her soul. The alchemy she has created is medicine—a balm for the soul groping in the darkness, a buffer against heartbreaks that linger in the mind.

Catherine's genius lies in the selflessness of these offerings. These are lyrics of love, an emotion she embraced with confidence and allowed to guide her. Just as she led her life giving to her family and friends, so she gave over to her muse. She welcomed the consolation of paper and pen in the middle of the night and in the hours of dawn and dusk. There she could open herself to the great unknown and listen. That listening has brought us hundreds of gems that continue to sparkle across time. Their light, their brilliance is needed now more than ever.

For she intuits that what is incarnate in land and sky, mountains and rivers reveals its presence in us, too. That numinous force, she affirms, will endure all the days of our life and beyond. With the daily flood of the world's anguish comes an unnamed luminescence hidden deep within the changing nature of things. It is here that she animates hope.

This volume appears as a distillation of her decades-long immersion in poetry. Her spiritual journey is lucid here, drawing on her depths of contemplation. It is emboldened by mystery, shorn of convention, and free of traditional religious language. This signals an invitation for the reader to enter into metaphors linking the mundane and the marvelous, moving from the particular to the universal. Here is the way of prayer.

She acknowledges that her poetry is a place where words enwrap us. Yet she brings us beyond language to a sensibility where words are no longer needed, where "a presence, nameless and unnamable breathes forth its power" ("Geography Lesson," p. 74). This is liberating, opening us to a space apart from tradition or scripture. Deftly, she draws us into fresh experiences and accessible intuitions, like a Zen koan resonating with life.

Her lyrical language ushers us gently into another realm of being, one where our consciousness is awakened beyond daily distractions. The fragmentation of existence is brushed aside for a moment and we catch a glimpse of that which is beyond the visible and yet apparent in the visible. The spontaneity of her imagination holds these poems together along with recurring themes that lure us in gradually—time and death, tragedy and loss, cosmos and nature, the unnamed and unknown.

In the end, her healing vision invokes a clear sense of living within deep time, subject to the unfolding dynamics of evolution that have birthed us. Here in "Waking in the Cosmos" she illustrates the identity we have with the cosmological powers and natural forces in which we dwell across time and space:

Within our blood
stars flash their signals,
rivers circuit their courses,
seas fluctuate rhythmically
while the dust of dead constellations
mingles with our bones.

Catherine celebrates our participation in the continuity
of being—from the smallest atom to the largest star. This
is what gives her work vitality in the face of loss and decay.
She has steeped herself in the sensuous beauty of Earth and
drawn in the vibrant powers of the cosmos so that we, too,
can abide in reverence and embrace renewal.

—MARY EVELYN TUCKER
Yale University

PROLOGUE

MUSE

"I shall not die,
   I shall not go away.
   Just don't ask me any questions,
   I shall not answer."
            —Ikkyû (1394–1481)

A full moon disk of hammered silver
appears in the east window
as the wind slowly rises in the woods
stirring the trees newly sheeted with leaves.
This is the hour of the night angel,
her pale wings rowing rhythmically
across the luminous evening.

What am I doing unfurling metaphors
as if anyone expects the tall ships of poetry
to roll up and offer safe passage
across strange seas? And yet the wind
still lifts great ribbons of song
from one side of the world to the other.

So I stand quietly on the quay of moonlight
and welcome the night angel, tender of gifts,
arriving from the outer reaches.

I

ANGEL OF SPRING

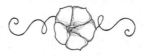

SPRING

When spring shakes open
the folds of her robe,
daffodils and violets fall out
petaling the brown earth
with pastels of light.
Where shall I be then?
Not counting the years,
but held in rapt attention
by the wafting scent,
by the wren, swallow, jay—
dashes of color ascending the sky—
going about their beautiful lives.
Nothing tentative here, a firm course,
an exact knowing of the direction
of air currents and wind streams.
I step outside of time
and lie down in fields of happiness—
What other name for what is nameless?—
and find myself made new again
in the ever greening world.

SUMMER

A white egret
floats across the blue sky
mirrored in the glassy water
where a tall heron
bends stiffly admiring
its reflection.

Nothing much,
yet enough to praise
the muskrat and the turtle,
enough to praise
the red wing and the goose,
above all enough to praise
the mothering power—
bearer of life beyond
the boundaries of mind,
the limits of language.

As the afternoon slides
into evening, I walk home
wrapped in darkness.
Behind the windows,
lamps open their corollas.
A slight wind, scented
with honeysuckle,
caresses my face.
Nothing much,
yet enough for joy.

FALL

"Praise this world to the Angel,
show him some simple thing."
—RILKE

Acorn:
a simple thing rolled underfoot,
little hat box,
container of ancient codes.
It needs only a handful of earth,
a cupful of rain, a slant of sun
to crack open, push forth a rootlet,
father a forest.

Can we arrange ourselves
in such a pattern?
Can truth spring forth,
can love leap from
some obscure place
in the sheltered heart?

To release the future
we let go, detach ourselves
from the mother-tree, fall
on the ground of our becoming:
we break open, spiral earthward
to tap the depths, reach skyward
to embrace the light.

WINTER

Winter repeats itself, writes
the same text year after year:
fox-printed snow,
ice-lacquered trees,
hours moving slowly
toward an evening of cold moonlight.
No sound but a train in the distance
passing through, as we all do,
bound to somewhere unknown.

Sometimes we think we are alone,
locked in the specifics—language, creed,
tribe. It isn't easy to say, "We the people,"
despite the same dreams, same delights.
With backpack slung over the shoulder,
we walk, walk, walk on, waiting
for the good omens of spring:
flags of green leaves released from the stem,
flashes of red wings released into the air.

We grow old, we are tired,
but never forget the fire burning
in the inner room of the spirit.
We keep the flames high,
adding to the blaze bits of paper,
poems, prayers.

THE BEAR

Blinding white
invisible in the light
she watches me.
For a long time
I have known her true name:
Death, White Death,
disguised under luxuriant fur.
She waits for me up north
at the confluence of pure rivers.
For a long time
I have said, "Yes, yes,
take my necklace, my ring,
take the soft round curve,
the bread-shape of my life.
Eat it with strong teeth
and drink what flows easy and quick—
the good wine of my love
poured out in libation on the stone."
Of course I am afraid,
but when you come for me,
my bright grunting angel,
I shall say, "Yes, bring me home
carry me beyond brambles and thorns
to that sacred place higher than silence
where God sings."

The Year Just Beginning, the Winter Half Gone

Downy soft
snow feathers the world
falls deep within the soul.

Slow motion of time: hours peel away
one by one, pages without text,
language without words.
Trapped in its sarcophagus
the past wears diadems and rings,
brocaded dresses, yellowed bones.

The present tries to forget
rumors of disaster, to ignore
the angel of death invading towns,
breaking doors, leaving in her wake
a trail of ashes and blood.

What passes through the hands:
strands of many colors,
beads, totems, amulets.
What passes through the mind:
images, thoughts, words
knotted into a narrative of life.

Constellations of ice on the window
map the crystallized silence.
Nothing moves but the hawk
flying low, hunting for prey.

Locked in our winter rooms
we lean toward the light,
toward a warm leafy future
where the red rose will bloom
again.

LUMINOUS MORNING

Breathing in, breathing out
the luminous morning air
passing through, always passing
from one day to the next.
In the distance the marsh reeds
crackle in the wind,
while just here the leafless wood drips
clear tree-thoughts after the rain,
its interlocked branches forming
an architecture of bones.

What are we doing in this place?
The years slip through our fingers,
coarse threads falling slack
on the ground of our lives.
Do we need to sorrow
for the ancient garden?
Paradise is not lost, it is here
offered, with its sentinel of angels,
its vigilant spirits, its sacred grove.

When death comes with her white cortege,
her chariots and plumed horses,
what shall we say, what words
to enunciate separation and distance?

Can we presume language will evolve
far enough to spell what has no name?
Time escorts us away, we pass
through its burning arcades
as ashes snow on our heads.
What is hidden beyond any measure,
beyond any articulation of belief,
is no less real than the crow
striding across the clearing
in its shiny black suit.

THIRST OF SPRING

Buds no bigger than pinheads
push through dark stems.
A bird sings,
as it has done for centuries,
clamped on the same twig
with the same black claws.
We are passing wanderers
suckled on sour milk:
what we drink is death
and what we eat is flesh
from great slaughtered beasts.

Have you seen the moon
salting the world to brightness
at midnight?
Have you heard the trees,
leaning mysteriously against each other,
clattering like Japanese clappers
when there is hardly any wind?
Have you felt life like a bolt of silk
unrolling from your shoulders?
Then yes, you can laugh
in this unlaughable universe:
you can laugh and walk home
with the greening world singing
in your heart, in early April,
on an ancient mountain.

Everywhere Rain

Everywhere rain, north and south,
rain with her long wet hair,
her heavy gray gown dripping
over the land. The day streams
and we sit in half darkness
while rain taps at the window
with her watery fingers.
We ask ourselves where to find
a place for the angel of light
when our thoughts begin to melt
and ripple down with the sound
of the wind-chased rain
clattering on the roof.
The whole world drip-drops
into the night. Tomorrow,
if the weatherman is right,
the sun will shake itself
free of the clouds and clarity
will return with its transparencies,
its sharp outlines, its crystalline fields.
And yet today, in the shadows,
in the small circumference of our lives,
the soft hands of rain
wash us clean of sorrows.

ANOTHER STORY LINE

If words shape truth–
small easy words, containers
of love's tender ache—
where is the text to be read?
At the table, in the street,
in half-lit bedrooms at night?

The earth speaks a language of clarity:
what is, is, without disguise or ambition.
Consider the lilies of the field,
consider how the trees always receive us
with the open arms of their branches.
They shelter, embrace, pacify—
the wind carries their leafy voices.

We reach out, try to connect
flesh to flesh, mouth to mouth,
to resurrect a narrative
we all hold in common.
We pour ourselves out,
decant our lives
into trivial pursuits
rising and falling
in and out of the light.

What happens
when the solemn angel of death
comes knocking at the door?
How do we answer?
With silence, denial, retreat?
Or do we discover another story line,
a pilgrim's way leading to communion,
prompting us to kneel down,
to kiss the beauty we call "God"?
Such a clumsy, spurious name
to enclose what is beyond knowledge,
beyond and within the limits of the heart.

A SMALL WINDOW

Sometimes a small window opens
in the mind and we see
neither a presence, nor an image,
but something magnificently essential,
impossible to translate or express.
Then we proceed, move ahead
the same way with the same tasks,
the days, the landscape unaltered:
the trees mantled in new leaves,
waving their green-sleeved arms
and the pink azaleas coloring the day.
A whole lexicon of renewal
defines the narrative of spring.
In the mind, the small window
does not close: we see life forever
ongoing past its boundaries
well beyond the darkness of death.

A Buried Seed

Their thick clusters full of bees,
the flowers of the catalpa flicker
like votive lights among the branches.
Already the wild roses are fading,
their seasons progressing
toward their red fruit.

Time slips away, slithers
down the path, a snake
shedding its mottled skin.
Nothing keeps still long enough
except the ancient rocks
and the old mother-turtle
brooding at the water's edge.
For millennia, the same equation:
familiar sky, same blue road
for the wandering sun.
And yet we pass, are passing,
pushed like clouds by the wind.

So many partings in the past:
the boat leaving the pier,
the diminishing figure of a father
waving, waving us on to another land.
In the train station, at the bus stop,
handclasps, kisses, last goodbyes
and then steam, speed, mist, the wheels
turning, the bells clanging into the future.

We spell the words, "life," "death,"
write them on the blank page
in medieval script entwined
with gilded leaves. In the margin,
scenes of dailiness, vistas
of a childhood garden—grapevine,
apple tree, rose bush.

The dream persists: solution to the riddle,
answer to all needs, but things fall away,
float away without return.
The catalpa tree is in bloom
and in the center of the world
a buried seed slowly matures,
opens, grows—never to end,
never to die.

SORROWS

They lay their ghosted hands
upon us, unnamed sorrows,
secrets whispered in the dark.
Retaining their power, they hide
deep in the flesh, deep in the mind.
Can we distance ourselves
from the angry child, the dying man,
the lover turning away, retreating
into a forest of pain?

A new season slowly arrives
warming the trees into leafy wonders.
Rain follows in its chariots of clouds
and one pale flower, a snowdrop,
lifts itself out of winter.

Sorrows do not depart, they drag
their heavy sacks over the years
leaving tracks in the soul.
They repeat their dark words:
betrayal, loss, defeat, death.
Yet we know, keep on knowing,
life is blessed, resurrected
over and again.

Spring Garden

Open like a book,
with snow still spread
in the margins,
the day lies flat, silent.
Nothing to read but a few prints:
tracks of the passing deer.
We are, so they say, soon
to vanish in the wind.
Dust to dust, so they say.

Already we imagine the ease
of spring: the grass green stitches
patching the tapestry of the field,

the earth breaking open,
releasing the seeds of life.

We will walk in the garden,
see the stone rolled away,
the white linen folded and hear
a voice closer than our heartbeat
calling our name.

LIFE RISING

Words arrive, wide-winged,
high-flying vectors guided
by season and sun.
They have the voice of the wind,
the color of open waters.
What happens when they follow
the curve of the earth,
enter places of desolation,
see death in her counting house
writing in an enormous ledger
numbers ever on the increase?

Here, daffodils lift their small lights
and in the pine tree mourning doves
endlessly repeat their mantra.
Time speeds up, people vanish
leaving behind bones in deep trenches,
signs engraved in ancient rocks.
Words still arrive, carrying messages:
"Life rises out of dark roots
ever keeps on rising
toward the spring of the world."

RESURRECTION

In the recesses of language
we look for words,
not soft buttery ones,
hard ones, angular constructs
to house the larger mysteries.
We dissect, probe, examine,
yet no answers are given as we ask,
"How does the full moon open
its white blossom in the night?"
"How does the caterpillar, wrapped
in its gauzy shawl, transform itself
into a luna moth with pale green wings?"
"How does the child in the womb
grow fingers and toes?" We do not know,
we do not know, we do not know,
but we hold one knowledge
without proof: on the brightest morning
of the world, ahead of us, calling us,
a young Jewish man comes out
of the cave of death, robed in light.

As We Know

As we know,
the earth is a tiny sphere
spinning in a frozen void,
orbiting an enormous star,
spiraling in a vast galaxy,
circling a black hole.
As we know,
we are soft flesh
following the sun's course
hour after hour, year after year.

We often hope for tomorrow,
but what does it bring?
After the book of snow closes,
winter departs, waving goodbye
with her icy hands.
Small spring pleasures arrive:
the first daffodils, the trees
unfurling their new flags.

As we know,
in our unknowing,
the substance of our days
will be weighed, its gravity
less than that of a feather
adrift in the shifting wind.

WE ARE THE ONLY ONES TO KNOW

The dark folds of wings
unpleat themselves
to catch the rising air
and wheel into the clouds.

Can anything be proven,
can anything be certain
in this spiraling galaxy?
We feel the weight of time,
a heavy yoke on our back.
Behind us, the door of the past
slams shut with brutal force.
And yet tomorrow will be born:
the reddish knobs of maple flowers,
the robin emerging rumpled
from the broken shell,
the child wet from the womb
of a thousand generations.

In the flux of years,
we walk on fragile frames.
We are the only ones to know
death waits at the corner,
not a mugger, an austere angel,
her soft hands tucked
into billowing sleeves.

In the meanwhile of the now,
resplendent in its feather dress,
the hawk glides away,
without knowledge, without fear.

LORD OF WILD VIOLETS

So pale, so quiet, until the wind arrives
from some deep place in the south
pushing mouthfuls of air into the world,
ruffling the daffodils, billowing
the deep sleeves of the pine.

Lord of spring, Master of life,
we longed for you as we listened to the winter
howling at the door, scratching the lintel
with nails of ice.

Lord of wild violets, Master of running waters,
we know, in the end, everything falls down
fatally struck by the whiplash of death.

In the vast solar stream
your golden body flows unimpeded
drawing all times, all things
through the trail of amazements.
We bow in the ceremony of praise
your light ever rising over and beyond
the trajectory of disasters.

How long for us to discover
that we proceed with you
from splendor to splendor?

WAKING IN THE COSMOS

"The taboo against identifying with nature
has been lifted. Star-time, earth-time speak
through us; we are their soul, sound and tongue
—the universe's strange attractors."
                    DAVID TOOLAN

Not alien, yet too vast to imagine,
    this place we call home,
    this solitary jewel,
    sapphire on the throat of space.
Do we have eyes for the patch of earth
    in the backyard?
Do we feel the power of roots
    pushing the single grass blade to
    the light?
Yet sometimes an archaic memory
    stirs us awake.
We remember we are not alone,
    orphans lost in planetary storms.
We swim breast to breast
    with other luminous bodies.
Within our blood
    stars flash their signals,
    rivers circuit their courses,
    seas fluctuate rhythmically
    while the dust of dead constellations
    mingles with our bones.

Turbulence, disorder, chaos define the necessity
  to translate the song of the ocean,
  to transect the arc of the sun,
  the orbit of the moon.
We are the voice of plants,
  of animals, of stones.
We speak for galaxies
  as well as for the common violet
  both sisterly near, both alive,
  wedded to our fleshy heart.

II

ANGEL OF SUMMER

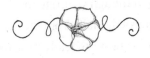

Summer

The morning-glories open
their lips reciting their blue name
the same, hour after hour,
until they shrivel by noontime
into little coffers of death.

We do not understand much
even though we pretend
knowledge falls from the sky
in soft heaps to feather the mind.
We do not understand words,
their meaning culled from millennia
evolving, twisting, rolling away
often lost with the changing tide.
Yet what we want to say
would break the glass of our ease:
news of war, famine, exile,
torture deepening in the heart
while the fiddler of death
plays his mournful tunes
and cities burn and towers slide
into ash and dust.
Our world, this world of discontent,
is where joy falls drop by drop—
a rare elixir slowly decanted
in small cups of memory.

Noon already.
The morning-glories close their lips,
end their blue incantations.
No word from the crow,
no word from the sun,
just a long, long sigh from the trees.

QUESTIONS

Questions dangle in the air
on filaments of silk,
compact little cocoons
hiding creatures of the night
dreaming of the light.

What you hear everywhere
in the streets, in public halls,
in closed rooms, "Why, why, why?"
People pleading, weeping in despair.
How easily sorrow fills the world.

Under the talon of the owl
high in the maple, something quivers
a shred of life torn by a dark beak.
Everywhere someone trembles and cries,
repeating the same word over and again,
while flesh bleeds, breath fails
and vanishing is not a magician's act,
but a distillation into nothingness.

And yet somewhere in the dark
a luna moth unfolds her luminous wings.

PETROGLYPH

Incised in the stone,
wavy lines, a script of sorts,
naming the age of the earth
beyond time, beyond the familiar.
If you think there is
no beginning, no god, no end,
then the world is just that:
no place, no story
no ceremonies, no rituals.
And yet if you can read
what is written in the stone,
the ridges carved
by millennia of sun and rain,
if you can see beyond
the flare of dying stars
burning in your bones,
then you belong
to the morning of the world,
then you stand at the confluence
of undivided kingdoms—
trees, rivers, mountains
inside and outside of history—
each as real, each as beloved,
as the other.

AN EXTRAVAGANT FUTURE

Not everything is written down
in plain script. Mystery,
like a magician's cloak,
covers what we cannot understand:
the traveling stars flashing
their already extinguished lights,
the child growing in the womb,
encoding the history of generations,
the trees leafing again on schedule
reclaiming their green power.

How can we account
for the ache and longing of life,
that deep unhealed wound,
that desire for wholeness, for joy?

Underground invisibly
water bubbles, rises to the surface,
begins to flow, to mirror the sky,
to feed plants, to let the deer drink—
their soft mouths making soft sounds.

Deep in the breast invisibly
fire burns, passion flares, spreads
and what can we do but dance
the ancient mating dance
in the center of the flame?

The wind has no shape, it moves with haste
from one side of the world to the other
carrying weightless clouds, the song of the rain,
the scent of foreign shores.

The air, the fire, the water offer
intimations of paradise,
small ripples in the current
transporting us beyond the edge of sight.
Enough to know we are arriving
slowly at another harbor to find
what we cannot even imagine:
an extravagant future, an encounter.

In the Dimension of Forever

The sun signals the hour
in the corner of the window,
an open flower of light
marking nine o'clock.
Today the world is blue
sky of Chinese enamel.
The morning-glory vines
filigree the hedge, their
delicate silk purses
gathering the wind.

We cannot step out of life,
shed our skin, peel off our thoughts,
leave the place where we are rooted.
Time flows on, watering the hours,
cascading into a void of silence:
days, months, years slowly counted
and quickly unremembered.
The past remains a set of images,
some vivid, some half erased.
Like old photographs
our stories are curled at the edge,
faded to dull colors.

In the dimension of forever
we are powerless to define
what is beyond the realm of the stars.
Today, the reality of our body—
heart, hands, tongue, eyes—
is fused, blessed with the cycles
of earth, air, fire, water.
No need to go anywhere:
we are here secure
in the already now of God.

ALREADY NOW

Sometimes our days are hard,
hard as the proverbial iron,
unrefined slag, cold and dark.
Sometimes our days are soft,
dressed in silk—close to the
skin the cloth falls in elegant
pleats down to our ankles.
Such is life, no straight lines,
only jagged edges, undulating curves
and the ever turning road leading
to the intersection where everything stops.

Mid-June. Blackbirds passing through
write their hieroglyphs in the sky.
Shadows of the pine trees kneel down
on the grass: images within images
ever transformed, ever retreating.

Yet we shall rise beyond stone and dust,
we shall hear voices singing the world alive.
We shall be quiet with the quietness of lovers
when silence covers all that was said.
Already now we are farther than the wind,
already now we are home.

WHO KNOWS WHAT HAPPENS IN THE DARK

At first you see nothing,
not even the outline of your thoughts.
Something formless, a scarf of night,
covers your eyes. Then, shadows
emerge through the trees,
owl-words begin to fly on cottony wings
and in the underbrush small animals—
hidden metaphors—scratch the soil
looking for seeds and snails.

You wait immobile, silent
until the rain begins to fall:
gray threads woven into a wet shawl.
You remember the sinuous body of rivers,
the tongue of the sea licking the shore.
You hear the stars chanting ancient lore,
the fox calling forgotten names.
Then you find your voice and you know
you too can sing.

THAT SINGLE WORD

Scrambled, the letters of the alphabet
rearrange themselves into cities of words,
dwellings for poets and singers,
gardens for children and cats.
We wander through the streets
looking for the altar of light,
the radiance at the center.
How many years did we squander,
changing direction, losing our way,
flittering here and there,
letting time go by, idle, soft at the edges.
We cherish the fancies of language:
active verbs strolling by,
trying to hook up with glittering nouns,
little adjectives gamboling merrily
through the text, adding color and sound
to a vocabulary pushing itself down
toward gray sidewalks.
In the center of the city, in the plaza,
a single word shines forth, a sun
ever rising through the debris of history,
spelling out what it means to be
woman, man, free.

FEEDING THE DEMON

Fear—
What is it you want?
The cords of my sinews,
my bones, my heart?
Standing at my side
you snarl in an alien tongue
I well understand.
You have long teeth
in an angular head
and you dog my steps,
nip my heels.
You are not singular:
your many children scamper
around me,
their cold snouts raising
the hair on my neck.
I will not strike you down
when you mimic a human cry,
I will chant the litany of your names:
fear of pain, fear of death,
fear of past, fear of future,
fear of burial in the snow
after tracking through eternal winters.
I will feed you by the kitchen door,
beggar that you are, the scraps
that fall from the table,

the crumbs of life's good bread.
I will feed you what mice and crow
do not want, what stirs at night
in the black cauldron of dreams.
Then I will send you away,
back to your dark lodging.
I will walk the garden path,
pluck the summer rose and
release the petals into the wind—
weightless, free.

AT WORK

I am building an altar
to the unknown God—
God of the pale moon,
God of the constellations,
God of the multitude,
all beloved, all enmeshed in mercy.
I am building a tower of praise—
each stone precisely cut, quarried
from the deep mine of language.
I am writing a canticle of thanksgiving
for the rain lacquering the world,
for the voice of the wind speaking
its long syllables to the trees,
for the iron wheel of time turning
joy and sorrow, life and death,
turning without pause.
Nothing can be omitted—
days added to days designed and colorized
according to the seasons.
I am offering thanks for the sparrow,
for the whale, the tiger, the antelope,
for the ant and the mouse, for the roses.
In the end, I will know, I will sing
the name of the unknown God
all things becoming transparent
to the light.

WE COME AND GO

We come and go, busy
with the dailiness of small tasks.
We know the time will come to cross
the bridge over the River Styx—
a long walk across a short span.
Yet some things never change:
the bending weight of summer heat,
the dry whispering of the wind
passing through the aspen trees.
We live hemmed in, held
within defined boundaries,
some visible, some not.
We cannot understand, stand under
what has no edges, no limits—
we come and go toward
an immense embracing splendor,
impossible to describe, where no one
is ever found wanting.

ON THE PILGRIM PATH

Morning. Sunlight stitching together
all we can see: house, tree, grapevine.
Sometimes we sleepwalk through the day,
not noticing the wind rising and falling,
not hearing the waterfall of words
cascading on the soul.

Death waits around the corner—
wrapped in dark robes, speaking
of distances impossible to measure,
chasms impossible to cross.
We stand here among the ephemera:
books in piles on the floor,
flowers nodding their short lives
on the table, photos of people, places
lost in the flux of time.

Whatever was written, text after text,
in the long unfinished story
remains incomplete, misted over
by the rains falling down, blurring
the narrative, covering the holy names
of all who breathe and walk
on the pilgrim path. The day will end,
stars will open their enormous corollas,
someone will turn the last page,
will close the book.

ZODIAC

"In my end is my beginning."
—T. S. ELIOT

The zodiac with its mythic beasts
turns its wheel in the night sky:
emblems printed in old books
with texts of forgotten lore.
Down here, under drifting clouds,
the clematis is in bloom,
some white, some blue, perishable,
caught, as we are, in time's revolutions.
We will not come back to this hour
added to the millennia of time.
What are we trying to say, then,
year after year, when all we know
dissolves into vapor and mist?
In a world of evolution, movement,
change even what rests
in the Chinese painting—
trees draped in black-laced finery,
water swathed in azure-hued silk—
will break down, transform
into other shapes, other meanings.
In the mirror on the wall,
our younger selves appear
with gray hair and stooped back.
And then somewhere
down the descending stair
time will stop its wanderings:
in my end is my beginning.

WHAT WE DO

Arrival, departure, and in-between
alternance of day and night.
So little can be told,
so little surmised from the shifts
from here and there, life and death.
What is real today will vanish tomorrow
into forgotten wastelands:
the glaciers melting into the sea,
the faces we love cold and stiff.
We are left alone on the beach, staring
at the years surging and falling away.

For a moment, stand still, read
what is written in the book of light,
how things shine and sing:
invisible music heard only
in the recesses of the listening heart.
Look at the tulips, how they smile,
how their red lips open in new chants.
Hear the steady mantra of water dripping
down from the eaves.

All the small gods—
money, power, fame—are dying.
We do not ask questions, do not answer
inquiries about age and fortune.
Instead we do what the old Buddhist monk
said to do: "Haul water, chop wood."

WHAT WE KNOW

Time always undoes itself,
letting the days fall
one by one into muddy waters.
No coming back, no return.
Raw life transmutes itself
into dry memories, nothing left
but artifacts—spoons, cups, plates—
all the detritus of the past.
We learn early the midnight of things,
how quickly they drift away, carried
by the sorrowing wind.
We are told to pray: How, when, where?
We repeat old incantations—nothing
but gray pebbles rolling underfoot.

Those who came before us, dressed
in their long coats and tight shoes,
knew something of stillness and silence.
They spoke another language, named
the constellations and felt the moon
pulling the tide of their blood.
Now glaciers break, slide into the sea,
the sound reverberating in our ears.
Now the name of God is an empty place
on the crowded calendar. "Ashes to ashes,"
we are told as the long lines of the poor
stream down the city streets.

Trapped in a million little boxes,
we yearn for distance, largess of love,
beauty without end.
Our footprints hardly mark the dust
and yet we believe, no, we know,
the light sharper than the sun's rays
remains undimmed. The single word
spoken at the beginning continues
to be heard in all things:
an immense respiration fanning out
through and beyond the edge of the world.

Pure Voices

Our knowledge of God
is a small box,
container of definitions,
conjectures, questions, rules.
We carry it day by day:
heavy as it is, we stumble
sometimes when we lift it.
In fair weather it is lightweight,
filled with strips of paper
printed with words
in an ancient language
no one can understand.

Many things are left unsaid:
secrets hidden deep
in the mind's dark places
away from time's arrhythmic
years, numbered, counted
in a narrative of gain and loss.

And yet there is no box,
only an immense chorus:
pure voices of earth, water,
air and light singing,
without commentary,
"Holy, holy, holy is the Lord."

ENIGMA OF THE WORLD

Empty window, empty frame,
emptiness of the world
when the ink of darkness spreads,
erasing contours and colors.
What was in plain sight recedes.
The night's heavy hand censors
the stars, redacts the moonlight.

Once upon a time, we sat
in the sun of our ease, far away
on a beach where the blue sea
unrolled its white scrolls.
We waited for the future to appear
bejeweled like a queen.
What happened to the dream?
On the table, empty cups,
books unopened, unread.

In the sequel: calligraphy of morning,
green script of new leaves,
the wind traveling vast distances
beating its great wings
against the soft edge of things.
Enigma of the world unresolved,
yet what we thought was lost
is found—we live forever
in the transparency of the light.

FRAGMENTS

How far
across the immeasurable distance?
Maybe a few paces or hand spans,
but what we find: immense wilderness,
waterways impossible to bridge,
filled with depths in which to drown.
How can we attain what we seek?

In the land of sorrow
language darkens: nouns, verbs
lie down, tired, depleted.
When it begins to rain, words drip
with long suppressed tears.
Yet it does not last: morning opens
its golden doors, the story revives
to new chapters and verses
and life flows on and on
well past its natural borders
and, yes, well beyond death.

Do not ask when or where
as if playing hide-and-seek
with children in a dark wood.
Questions are frail constructs
built with twigs and straw.
Comes the storm and nothing

remains but mud and slugs.
Accept the mystery of death,
the unknown dialect impossible
to decipher, accept the passageway
without markers or signs.

TOPOGRAPHY OF THE WIND

We want to learn the topography
of the wind, watch it whistle
across the sea, arriving breathless,
weakened, from miles away.
We want to return to the snowdrops
of early spring, in another land.
Nobody around, the war distant,
noiseless. How many years ago now?

Time passes by in heavy boots,
its tracks quickly vanishing.
The witnesses leave, their words
forgotten, their names erased
from the big book.
What remains: an altar of offerings,
flowers in an ancient garden,
star patterns—dots, dots, dots—
crystals in the night.

The mind explores the outer reaches,
the soul stretches to the edge of the map.
Comes the hour in a nowhere to be seen,
someone speaks our name, calling us
beyond the blue ridge of the world,
beyond the future.

Our Father Not in Heaven

Our Father not in heaven,
present here in our plight,
hallowed be your name,
your unknowable name,
hidden in the roots of plants
in the calyx of flowers
in the throat of night.

Father not in heaven, you walk
in the land of hungry children,
in the streets where women are sold.
You cross the dangerous seas
in fragile rafts, in leaking boats.
You lie on the bed of illness,
in cancer wards, in refugee tents.
Your kingdom has come,
kingdom of rags and bones,
tears and wounds,
a reign of crucified love.

Father, your hand of mercy
parts the shadows, touches
all that is bitter and broken,
touches us like silk, like oil.
You move through our dreams
tattooing our soul with hope.
Father not in heaven, your story
unspools its golden thread,
its silver ribbon and your love
weaves round us a garment of light.

III

ANGEL OF FALL

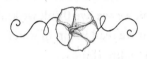

FALL

Flaming red in the early morning light,
the Japanese maple releases to the wind
its calligraphy of leaves. In its house
of grass the one-note cricket falls silent.

Beyond the absolutes of fact
there is a world we do not understand.
We think we see, we think we know,
but what we read in air, in water,
in earth, in fire shines
with a trembling light.
We observe, analyze, probe,
but we cannot reach the essence
of what it means to be woman, man,
of what it means to be fox, turtle.
Even a simple stone is an enigma,
a lost piece of a larger text.
Attempts at definition end
in scrambled words gathered
into naked shivering phrases.

We strive to enter the mystery,
the inner courtyard, prelude to revelation.
We imagine walking past the chimeras,
past the bronze demons and jade dragons.
We imagine walking down the long corridors
of prayer and finding at last an open door
and touching, being touched, by splendor.

HOW TO PRAY

Hard work at first: silence, solitude,
thoughts reeled into quietness.
No sound but the hum of emptiness.
No words, locked as they are
in their black script, unable
to translate the maple's golden aura,
or to reach the far distance,
the zone remote, unknown,
yet closer than our breath.

How can we pray?
The broken world weeps
tears salted with anguish.
Time never rests,
it tick-tocks our lives away,
the years strictly numbered,
each one named:
the year of the ox,
the year of the dog,
the year death entered the house—
a radiant angel dressed in silks.

No need to recall the past,
to brush the crumbs
off the table of history.
How to pray: be still
and in your stillness
dance.

Nothing More to Say

Sometimes the world shrinks
to vacancy, to husk and dusk.
Sometimes it's hard
to stand upright, to listen
to the small voices whispering
in the leaves, in the wind,
in the water falling over the rocks.

Among still visible things, wild violets
turn their azure eyes toward the setting sun.
In the woods, life pulses its green light
and the resident fox appears,
a red letter in the text of the evening.

Nothing left to say. At nightfall
the poem hangs upside down
in the rafters of the imagination.
It dream-sleeps, waiting for moonrise,
waiting for the moment of awakening,
the moment of ecstatic flight.

REJOICE AND BE GLAD

Silence:
no bird, no wind, no word
only the stillness of late night
and the moon's imprint on the grass.
Yet one hears the perpetual question
rising from under the ground,
from fossil shells, amber beads,
old bones. They keep telling
the same story—a procession
from pulsing star to plum tree,
to the beak of the finch.
How to unravel the ragged weave—
knots and twists, gains and losses—
of our tangled history?
We all carry secrets, untouchable memories.
We all wear a cloak of sorrow spread
in dark folds across the shoulders.

"Rejoice and be glad," sang the Psalmist
in a land of heat and thirst.
In the curve of earth's silence
we are cradled, mothered,
rocked to sleep.
Soon, the rains will come.

INDIAN SUMMER

Sometimes nothing needs answers—
can you imagine anything more beautiful
than the eternity of this moment?
The sun, Etruscan gold shining
in an enamel sky,
the purple aster swaying
in the warm wind,
the newborn child opening
her eyes to the universe.
Some days all things look perfect,
not to be altered,
not to be labeled,
not to be touched.
Who can understand,
who can stand under the old questions
when the woods vibrate with cicadas
and time stands still listening
to the earth's ancient song?

It does not last:
in the city, ciphers stand guard
over great sums, the numbers
to be counted over and again,
to be locked in boxes and vaults.
Soon the mind begins to turn its wheels,
to put forth its whys and hows and whens,
forgetting to account for the rose
bending its pretty pink head
in prayer.

LUNA

Silently, wearing silver slippers,
she walks in the garden.
The fox follows her trail,
the owl calls her with one note.
She is Queen of the Night—
not a patch of plaster
spackling the sky.

Do we know we are one
with all that lives and breathes:
grass, fern, aster
and even the golden beetle
burrowing in the earth?

Daily we hear about losses,
the litany of disasters:
hungry children, weeping women,
cities collapsing into rubble.
Are we going to destroy this world,
this holy gift, our home?

The moon appears at the window,
glides into the room, waves
her wand of light across the floor.
We watch her for a while,
her radiant round face:
Beautiful Luna,
Queen of the Night.

GEOGRAPHY LESSON

In the geography of the text,
mountains and valleys, cities and villages,
while between the words elaborate roadways
lead to further inquiries.
We walk down the sentences
where verbs and nouns stand guard
at the gate of meaning.
Out of the familiar vocabulary
we draw an alphabet of connectives,
chain-links between past and present.

In the geography of the map
the dragon flips its tail
twists its scaly coils
around the continents.
It isn't dead—the great serpent
in its greenish armor still lifts its
flat head above the waves
disrupting the flow, muddying the work.

In the geography of the poem
a presence, nameless and unnamable
breathes forth its power.
Through the curves of language
a voice speaks, soundless yet filling
the world with resonance.

Later, long after the last geese
arrow south, piercing the horizon,
who will read the fragile signs on the paper,
who will decipher the hieroglyphs
penciled in faded notebooks?

When the story is complete,
written in flesh and bone,
the voice will continue to chant
singly in the multiplicity of time.
After our long traveling, after our toil
we shall arrive at the end of the line
enter a space beyond parenthesis
where the incense pot glows
where the smoke rises and curls
upon the last stop.

LONG DAY'S JOURNEY

Traveling by train
watching the landscape sliding by:
squat houses, flat meadows,
miniature cattle in the distance
ghosted by mist.

Hours, days, years glide away
as we ponder the enigma of time:
the past impossible to retrieve,
its images dissolving in the mind,
the future impossible to predict.
its whispers scattering in the wind.
Wedged in-between only this moment,
caught in the staccato of the rails, remains.
Where are we going, to what altered place,
what country of the imagination?

We know our destination:
at the end of the line,
at the last station,
someone waits for us.
She calls our name,
we enter her embrace.

NOW

Flowing downstream
on that cliché, the river of time,
we clutch dried flowers,
creased letters, old books
our memories reduced
to a few faded photographs.

What is the measure of life,
how many fathoms deep?
Easy it was to live
in the abundance of leafy days
before winter spread its icy shawl
across our tired shoulders.
And yet we keep the company
of witnesses, the past of configurations.
"Now," says the child emerging from the womb.
"Now," says, the daffodil lifting its trumpet.
"Now," says the wind shaking the world.

In our mind's eye we see our future
unfold on the altar of light:
death, yes; resurrection, yes;
transformation in new fields of love, yes.
"Now," says the Lord.

AXIS MUNDI

Sunset.
You start here, at the end of the story,
where words no longer plumped with meaning
fail to encompass the larger mysteries.

Nightfall.
We are afraid.
What if the ancient texts
found in the desert sands are hollow
bells without clappers?
What if death is only a box of bones,
a stony silence no one can break?

Sunrise.
The darkness of unknowing recedes
and we are given fresh sight.
Beyond hesitant belief
we know: that man who was dead
is glorious alive—*axis mundi*—
his love, flames that do not burn.
We are not afraid.

HOME

Night sky, ash gray, starless
and the bed, a small wooden boat
anchored in the mythology of dreams.
In the morning we wake to disorder,
breakage, unexpected dread.
We hear death playing her fiddle
outside, under the window.
We listen, know the tune, feel
the knee of fear pressing on our neck.
Will it destroy the scaffold of life built
so long ago—house of flesh and bone
filled with ancient stories?
In the garden, flowers ring their blue bells,
trees wave their long arms, repeat
in leafy semaphore the wind's message.
No need to take to the road—
we are home in past, present, future.
We will live safe and well
in the light of the everlasting sun.

LISTEN

Listen:
a small voice cries in the wind
as the destroyers march on,
crushing innocent lives, nailing
the wrists and feet of the beloved.

Do we ever know where we are going,
to what destiny, what geography,
what hours of darkness, of light?
Time runs on, days dissolve
in long sequences, shape
landscapes of sorrow, vistas
of history: war, hunger,
the loneliness of despair.

Deep inside us another voice
chants the children's songs
we learned early in Eve's garden.
Pay attention!
See the world tenderly held
in the body of God, made of earth
of flesh like ours
of human beauty like ours.
He moves on ladders of air
ascending beyond the sky's limits
yet always descending to be seated
at our table, eating, drinking, blessing
the bread and wine of our toil.

No past or future here,
only the infinite present, a longing,
pulsing with the rhythm of our blood.

How a Poem is Born

Midnight. Deep darkness.
No stars to be seen,
only the wind moves
humming in the trees
with a plaintive note.
Words, brittle with age,
are silent, hidden in old books.
Suddenly, out of the blue,
something happens:
the angel of the hour arrives,
bright-winged, radiant.
She opens her immaterial mouth
and sings: the poem is born.

ORPHEUS

We count, recount,
add and subtract,
yet the sum always
remains the same.
Numbers stand stiff guard,
barring the door to life.
Hope rises, dressed in frills,
then collapses and fades.

Then, we cross over
to another landscape
where the tower of ciphers
no longer shadows our lives.
Orpheus did not die,
he still sings on the riverbank,
songs of freedom and beauty.
We follow his voice,
harmonize his words
that open the door
to the dance of wild things
unaccountable.

HISTORY

History is always with us
in all its disguises—
from filthy rags to finest silks.
It cannot be closeted,
locked in an ancient armoire.
Actors, or bystanders, we watch,
often weep, as the follies parade
unstoppable. We follow down the road,
spinning our little tales, our lacy poems
so fragile, so easily broken.
We wonder where we are heading,
to what otherness of life,
what other season's cycles.
Then someone else appears,
opens a path, reveals the place
where history is transfigured,
where children, poets, musicians
dance by the river of light.

RADIANCE

In the hourglass
sand trickles down
slowly without pause.
One by one, the hours drop
in a void, never to return.
Some fall hard, like stone upon stone,
others melt away, like a soft rain.

What can be done when doubt,
that mangy dog, digs up the yard?
Better to be quiet, let it growl
and look instead at the honeysuckle
its golden throat drinking
in the sun.

Year after year, it comes to pass:
time without shadows,
life rising, an astral body
without name or address,
radiance without end.

ANCESTRY

They are many,
those who came before,
migrating through millennia
to reach us.
They traveled,
people of the forest,
people of the hills,
rested in camps,
settled in caves.
They carved bone flutes,
painted ochre animals.

The past always waits at the door
wearing odd clothes, claiming attention,
recording gains and losses.
Note by note, the ancient chants,
incantations fill the soul.

End of September here: the bees
guard the hive replete with honey,
the wren bobs farewell to the rose,
and we hear stories on the news
of carnage, famine, landslide—
death stalking the land.

And yet in the great invisible assembly,
above and beyond the daily traffic,
small steady voices—angels, children,
poets—continue to sing of life renewed
and holy.

LORD OF SILENCE

No answer as we call
only a loud harsh wind ferrying
clouds across the sky.
You, Lord of Silence, remain
undeclared: hidden splendor
radiant absence-presence.
We move on through the years,
often on bleeding knees,
from one place to another.
Time never ceases to drift
filling space with watery mist.

Is it the head or the heart
where memories remain alive—
caged birds with clipped wings?
We cannot return to the land
where long ago we unpleated
life's many folds
to stretch ourselves into the light.
Better not to look back.
The future, still transparent,
opens its glass doors. We enter
terra incognita where you,
Lord of Silence, dwell.

ANOTHER STORY

"Beauty will save the world."
—DOSTOEVSKY

Bad news in the West:
fire shakes its flames over the land,
snakes and liars slither into the open
and assume power.
Bad news in the East:
war, illness, hunger, earthquake,
the needle of death sews a shroud.

Another story is told
down the ages, each to each:
beauty will save the world,
she of the soft hands, open in blessing.

Can you see the mother cradling her babe?
Can you hear the sound of silence
slowly shaping prayers?
Can you listen to the bluebells,
their azure tones ringing in
a colorful new day?

Life rises from the stone,
voices sing in the abyss.
Everything we touch has a shining,
for light never dims on the pilgrim's way.

IV

ANGEL OF WINTER

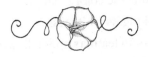

WINTER

The sun burns on its high altar,
the ice crackles underfoot
and we dress our bones
in the wool of language.
We chat about the weather,
rate the wind's velocity,
define the color of snow–
linking its whiteness
to swan feathers, moon flowers
and the bridal gown folded
in the hope-chest of dreams.
And yet beyond our words
an echo lingers, a pure sound,
the square root of all music
transecting the distance.

A MYSTERY OF ANGELS

Between this and that a gap
through which angels glide–
angel of spring, angel of fall,
angel of summer, angel of winter–
invisibly white, burning with light.
Abstractions? Possibilities?

Around us, the certainty of shape:
the thick walls of the house,
the hard wood of the doors,
the broad ferns of the ice
spreading across the windows.
And yet we feel raw, unsheltered,
in our soft flesh, shivering
with fear, threatened over and again
in a land of wind and storm.

Lighter than air
the angel of winter arrives
delivering celestial messages
in alphabets of snow.
Time overtakes us: moment by moment
the future, unrehearsed, comes in
escorted by a cloud of witnesses,
a mystery of angels.

THE EMBRACE OF MYSTERY

Where? How? When?
Questions pulse in the mind,
velvety moths looking for exits
to escape into answers.
We gather the years, each one tagged,
inscribed with our name
in the book of fear.
We wonder: where are we going
with our thin wrists, our fragile bones?
What will happen to the polished amulets
we keep in deep drawers of memory:
secrets, sorrows, desires and the scent
of lilacs in the spring?

Wedged between the astronomy of sky
and the geography of earth,
we ever wonder about our fate.
We live our lives and our stories
write themselves, the chapters added
one to another like stones paving a road
to an unknown destination.
In the end, words tumble into silence
as reality enlarges into mystery.
In the gift of its embrace
we see a multitude of answers
we no longer need.

VISITOR

You enter the room,
Angel of Death, with folded wings.
You are the color of light
as it rises in early morning.
Bodiless, without footprints,
but with eyes bright-seeing,
you reach beyond past and future.
With tender hands parting the shadows,
you gather all the folds of life,
uncovering what was forgotten or lost.
How quiet you are, how empty of desire.
You know our names, call us one by one
from great distances, yet stand close
enough to touch the center of our heart.
You enter the room,
open your translucent wings
and lift us, lighter than air,
into infinite configurations of love.

CONFLUENCE

Sometimes I forget
what I said
half a century ago
in the gray dust of war:
"No," in the winter rain,
to the man I loved–
a Star of David hidden
under his coat.
I moved away,
crossed the ocean,
built a house full of children
while he still waited
in the night of long ago,
the light of the streetlamp
streaked with rain falling
on his beloved face.
I was young, beautiful, blond.
He was not my lover,
only a man who loved me,
wanted to walk with me
into the future. I was fated
elsewhere on a different path.
The years built their walls,
yet I always remember
what I wanted to say long ago
in a time of darkness and fear:
"Yes, yes, yes, we shall meet
again."

JANUARY

After a glacial beginning
life paves the year day-by-day.
In the storybook we hear
the footfalls of many summers,
listen to the children singing,
conjuring twinkling little stars.
Centuries go by much traveled
by merchants, pilgrims, armies.
We hobble along on broken,
scuffed shoes, carrying burdens
from one country to the next,
while time continues its fast march
down ever narrower roads.

January returns: the black sticks
of winter trees bend low, snow-tipped,
counter-balanced under the icy moon.
What is the color of tomorrow?
In our dreaming, darkness opens
its mouth and out comes a cascade
of roses: the wolves in the hills
are lying down with the sheep
and the wind speaks in tongues
telling good news of peace.

And yet, as we wake, we see
breakages, pain, mortality—
angels fall and the abyss roars.
Shall we endure, Lord, shall we stay
silent through stormy weather?
Shall we pray?

ANOTHER WINTER

Another winter, another long trek
into silence. In the living room,
on the shelves lining the walls,
even the books are voiceless,
their words, little dark mummies,
lie wrapped in dried meaning.
In the garden, angels of snow
descend, spreading on the ground
the wide folds of their wings.

In the month of the hungry moon
the narrative of life can be read:
hieroglyphs printed in the snow,
signatures of the night visitors—
deer, fox, rabbit—passing through,
their destination never in doubt
as they follow their ancient trails.

Where are we going, in what direction?
The answer cannot find us living
as we do in the fluctuations of time.
And yet we can remember, we can learn
to be faithful to the summons of art,
to be still in the stillness of winter,
to know the eternity that is always now—
a constant blossoming, an everlasting
ripening of possibility.

SITTING QUIETLY

"Our trouble comes from our inability
to sit quietly in a room."
                    —PASCAL

Obsessed with time
we look at the watch
strapped to our wrist.
One by one the hours retreat,
falling away, never to return.

From year to year we light
candles on the altar,
our lives rising with the flame
burning brightly, burning out.

Each day as we speak
verbs and consonants mesh
into a network of oracles:
tomorrow autumn will burnish the trees,
tomorrow ice will film the pond,
tomorrow the fish will swim in transparency,
tomorrow the wind will carry the leaves,
tomorrow winter will enter the woods
wearing her ermine coat.

What shall we do then, locked
in snow and silence?
Ignore the clock, stop
time's incessant chatter,
sit quietly in a room
and declare the name of love.

COMING SOON

For a moment, forget it:
the absence, the night without echo,
the spidery hours unrolling their silk.
Forget how time collapses its towers,
how they sink into crackling dust.
We fold the chairs of summer,
begin to count the syllables
forming icy words of winter.
Two plus two will always be four,
but numbers cannot account
for the last rose opened wide,
its pink lips curled by the wind.
No magic in the past, gone is gone
and what is left lingers
bittersweet on the tongue.
Now is the ground of our living,
now is the present without scars,
the morning opening itself
into bright blossoms of light
cancelling darkness.

SUMMARY

Days:
Some speak harsh words,
others ring like a glass tapped
by an indifferent finger.
Some brush against the face,
angel feathers plucked out of the sky
for no reason, no reason at all.

Years:
They pass, are passing,
freight trains rumbling in the night
carrying summer boxes, winter loads.
They cannot stop:
the lights at the station are out,
the schedule hurtles ahead.

Life:
Additions, subtractions,
past and present divided,
a line no one can cross.
Voices can still be heard dimly:
fathers, mothers, children calling,
waving, as the long cars of memory
glide into the distance.

Time:
Fragrances lost, images faded,
sounds less and less intelligible.
At the end, the counting is done.
By an unknown gate, someone waits,
someone who knows our name.

THE PATH OF SILENCE

Old words, tired, used up,
lying down in their faded dresses,
sleeping in the pages of empty books.
Sometimes they wake in the imagination,
re-arrange themselves in new patterns.
One morning they spell snow, printed
with deer tracks, another morning
they chatter about the price of milk.
We want to break down the fence
where the alphabet is penned,
yet we cannot reach the corolla of stars,
we do not know how the sleet falls
in icy parallel lines. All life long
we travel from one question to the next,
gathering evidence, clues, adding words
to the great pile, the debris of our search.
If we take the path of silence, renounce
the drone of endless speech, the whine
of idle commentary, then someday
in a place that is no place, we shall see
without actual sight, pure essence,
real presence.

OPEN THE GATE

We look ahead, see the bright mirage
time of peace, of creative living.
Yet nothing happens but black terror:
the stream of exiles rejected,
sent into the desert night.
History, it is said, repeats itself,
but additions occur, new ways
to define disaster and death.
What happens when darkness falls
in sharp degrees of pain?
Where to go, where to hide?

The garden is calm: the deer crosses
the lawn, the hawk clutches the branch
and the wind lies almost still,
quietly breathing in the woods.
And yet there is no detour to take,
to avoid what lies outside, far away.

We turn and return to the sights:
ruined cities, wounded people.
Among the refugees, a young
Jewish woman in flight with her
unborn son. Open the gate.
Yes, there is still room at the inn.

CHRISTMAS

Nothing left but husks, twigs
and the wind, whipped by snow,
repeating itself: wolf-like howlings
passing through the arches of centuries.
The past, a moment frozen in ice,
the future, a vaporous ghost
supplier of dreams and fears.
What about the present? A swirl
of pleated air, a dervish of death.

In the expanding universe
all things move out, travel away
from their cloistered places–
we cannot alter their course.
Meanwhile, under indifferent eyes,
the glaciers are actually melting,
the sea outflows its borders,
the land bleeds, bitten deep
by the steel jaws of machines.

On the other side of time,
not much to hear: a heartbeat,
a newborn's cry, a singular word
speaking itself into impermanence,
announcing the immediacy of life
the sweet taste of it on the tongue.
Unknown to us, angels descend
down ladders of light, singing
of peace, their winged voices
lifted shining into the night.

WINTER NIGHT

Snow, full moon, stars—
winter night, unrepeatable time.
Down the millennia
clouds unfurl their billows
in the watery air,
seas unscroll their waves
on the papery sand.
The days float by one by one,
their sounds falling to a whisper.
Hellos and goodbyes
merge in a single moment.
We strive to remember,
but what was yesterday
sinks formless into the mist.
In the mirror of history,
ancestral faces smile,
mouth our names,
while time pulls our sleeve
eager to bring us forward.
Where? To the end
of our wandering?
Yet here we are, halfway
in winter snow, halfway
in the inner space where
love forever blooms
opening itself, offering itself,
fragrant as a red rose.

A SMALL FLICKERING LIGHT

Sometimes the mind turns north,
looks into the icy lands and sees
nothing—only glistening surfaces,
paw prints here and there and a ridge
where a fox's tail brushed the snow.

We live inside pockets of frozen air
in a desert bereft of the color of hope.
The century curves, closes its iron clasp
and inside its circling years history
wanders wrapped in death's black coat.
In the newspaper words bleed terror,
famine, war while prophets are chained,
oracles silenced and the wind lifts
a powder of ashes over the earth.

Who will return us to the garden's
mossy path where the jasmine blooms
and the benevolent lion lies
with the beneficent lamb?
Dream, illusion! Every day the sun
sails through the sky in a radiant barque
while the sound of agony rises,
growing in intensity, bursting through
the doors and windows of ruined houses.
Yet something persists
a knowing beyond names and facts
pierces the fleetness of time,
a small flickering light
enough to see beyond the dark.

TOUCH AND SEE

"Everywhere we find ourselves invaded
by the world of the sacred."
　　　　　　—THOMAS BERRY

Another winter:
slow rhythm of snowy days, slow traffic.
Two birds, smudges in the pine tree,
hungry, no doubt, and cold.
All around us definitions,
explanations of the unexplainable,
the world full of ruins and ashes.
And yet sunlight ripples through the woods,
the frost inscribes the windowpane
with its sparkling alphabet
and the sparrow does not fall
sustained as it is in flight.
These are not the last things
to be pressed under memory's glass,
these are the first things,
the simple, the obvious.
"Touch and see," says Wisdom,
"read the letters written
in the air, in the stones,
in the paw prints of foxes.
Listen to what is spoken in the heart:
the murmur of the past,
the golden claims of the future.

Hear the voices of the earth
speaking of sacred things."
No abstractions here, just the reality
of what is shaped, form upon form,
by the hands of God and inspired
with his breath.

AFTER THE FOUR SEASONS

Faceless, silent, unknown
God—a word without context.
In the present tense, simple things:
the faucet dripping day-after-day,
the rain tapping its wet code
on the roof of the world,
the wind muttering its ancient dialect.

In the morning paper
thousands perish, their ghosts
haunting us with their stories
and thousands are born luminous
beings ready to invent the future.

Nothing much changes:
same obstacles, same barricades,
same flaws, same mistakes.
Time, wearing its necklace of years,
quickly disappears around the corner.

After the four seasons, a
brief summary of life—
a few words on the page,
a scattering of dust.
On the last stretch of meaning,
nothing left but the light
transparency of the dawn
rising beneath our closed eyes.

GO HOME PILGRIM

"O you who have set out on the pilgrimage,
where are you going? The beloved is here, is
here living right next to you."
                                        —RUMI

Everything in flux:
years flow on and on,
some high tides, some low.
We follow their watery drift.
Landscapes change, languages evolve
losing words and meaning.
And yet questions retain their sting:
Where? Why? How? When?
Answers sometimes stiffen into laws
ignorant of shifting currents.

We hunger, we thirst,
wish for lodging, for humble meals.
Days are empty: no movement,
no color, no sound, only time
ever clocking its wandering.
Why the need to measure the distance,
to consult the stars—those nails of light
holding up the fabric of the night?
No need to travel. Go home pilgrim.
What you seek is here, is now, closer to you
than the wind caressing your face.

EPILOGUE

ANGEL OF THE LAST DAY

I stand on the quay of moonlight,
    then I run.
Where am I going?
    I do not know.
I look for the horizon,
    but see only a vast distance
    of undulating waves, impassable night.
I am afraid.
    Time trickles to a few grains of sand.
I settle here and there finding places to rest,
    to chant the tidal rhythms of prayer.
Then, someone arrives: a luminous being,
    angel of the last day.
She lifts her wings,
    I enter her embrace.

IRON
PEN

"O that my words were written down!
O that they were inscribed in a book!
O that with an iron pen and with lead
they were engraved on a rock forever!"
—*Job 19:23–24*

Outcast and utterly alone, Job pours out his anguish to his Maker. From the depths of his pain, he reveals a trust in God's goodness that is stronger than his despair, giving humanity some of the most beautiful and poetic verses of all time. Paraclete's Iron Pen imprint is inspired by this spirit of unvarnished honesty and tenacious hope.

OTHER IRON PEN BOOKS

ABOUT PARACLETE PRESS

PARACLETE PRESS is the publishing arm
of the Cape Cod Benedictine community,
the Community of Jesus. Presenting a full
expression of Christian belief and practice,
we reflect the ecumenical charism of the
Community and its dedication to sacred
music, the fine arts, and the written word.

SCAN
TO
READ
MORE

www.paracletepress.com